MONTH-BY-MONTH

Arts & Crafts

SEPTEMBER · OCTOBER · NOVEMBER

Compiled and Edited by Marcia Schonzeit

SCHOLASTIC
PROFESSIONAL BOOKS

New York · Toronto · London · Auckland · Sydney

To my son Sam,
a swell cutter and paster.

No part of this publication may be reproduced in whole or in part, or stored in a retrieval system, or transmitted in any form or by any means, electronic, mechanical, photocopying, recording, or otherwise, without written permission of the publisher. For information regarding permission, write to Scholastic Inc., 730 Broadway, New York, NY, 10003.

Designed by Nancy Metcalf
Production by Intergraphics
Illustration by Terri Chicko, Joe Chicko and Stephanie Pershing

Cover design by Vincent Ceci
Cover photography by John Parnell

ISBN 0-590-49123-7

Scholastic Inc. has made every effort to verify attribution for each of these ideas. Scholastic Inc. regrets any omissions. The ideas were compiled from *Instructor* magazine.

CONTENTS

SEPTEMBER   7

Get the year off to a good start with back-to-
school ideas and projects that help students get
acquainted. Honor Native American Day with
authentically inspired crafts. Throughout the
month share adventures in puppetry, clay, collage, design, and more!

OCTOBER   29

Celebrate fall with nature crafts and projects
that use easy-to-find materials. Imaginative projects for School Lunch Week, Columbus Day,
and other events lead the way to Halloween,
when imaginations really take off!

NOVEMBER   51

Start Thanksgiving celebrations with classroom
decorating projects. Turn ordinary materials
into extraordinary turkeys, Pilgrims, still-life
spectaculars, and centerpieces to take home.

Using This Book in Your Classroom

Month-By-Month Arts & Crafts offers you more than 50 classroom-tested, illustrated suggestions for every month of the school year. Because most of these projects were submitted to *Instructor* magazine by teachers just like you, you'll find them teacher friendly, success oriented, and appealing to a wide range of ages and abilities. Designed to promote individual creativity, the activities will please you as well as your students. Keeping in mind the needs of today's classroom, these arts-and-crafts experiences rely on inexpensive, easy-to-obtain materials. The emphasis is on simplicity, minimal fuss, and the fun of creating.

The activities, categorized by month, range from back-to-school ideas in September to fresh, new Thanksgiving suggestions in November. Seasonal projects celebrate major holidays and highlight other special events every month. In addition, there are ideas for bulletin-board displays and class projects as well as opportunities to experiment with such techniques as collage, papier-mâché, painting, puppetry, and drawing.

Many of the projects also integrate other curriculum areas. Working out a quilt design, for example, or determining how to assemble the elements of a class mural involves mathematical concepts. Having students tell a story about their drawing establishes a language arts link. And social studies tie-ins occur naturally as part of activities that celebrate birthdays of inventors, presidents, and other national figures. Scientific principles are implicit in experiments with watercolor techniques or drawing from observation.

A resource section on page 70 suggests background information and sources of inspiration to spark projects from paper folding to weavings based on Native American design principles. Finally, the index presents activities in alphabetical order, with special listings for major holidays.

Evaluating an art-and-crafts project is no longer limited to judging whether or not a child is "good" at art. More important is the expression of each child's unique view of the world. Experiencing the joy of seeing and the pleasure of creating are goals worth encouraging. Through these projects children learn to experiment without worrying about the "right" answer. They learn to expand their imagination. And they learn nonverbal ways to express themselves.

At the beginning of the year you may want to establish a link between school and home. A reproducible Letter to Parents on page 6 of this book enables you to enlist help from home in assembling scrap materials of all kinds. After your students have completed the activities in each of the *Month-By-Month* books, invite parents to an exhibition of the children's projects. Involve the class in displaying the artwork, taking home invitations (see page 57 for inviting invitations) and conducting tours through the gallery. Encourage home displays, too, with holiday gifts and other take-home ideas.

We hope that *Month-By-Month Arts & Crafts* provides you and your students with many hours of creative pleasure.

Letter to Parents

You might make copies of this letter and hand them out to your students during the first week of school. You can save time and paper by highlighting the objects you need as the projects come up. Remind your students to return the letter with the material from home. Place the letters in a file until you're ready to send them home again. Don't write any names on them—that way you can redistribute them.

Dear Parent:

We need your help!

Our class needs the following items for our arts-and-crafts projects. Please start saving them now, and I'll let you know when we'll need them.

Due Date

1. paper towel rolls
2. toilet paper rolls
3. magazines
4. soup cans
5. pieces of cloth, fabric scraps
6. ribbons, yarn, string, rope
7. cardboard boxes
8. old greeting cards
9. paper plates
10. wire coat hangers
11. clean Popsicle sticks
12. other:
13. craft materials you'd like to share with us:

Thanks,

SEPTEMBER

Get-acquainted projects for September include a class friendship wreath, colorful desk hangings, and self-portraits in several mediums.

Celebrate Native American Day with authentically inspired crafts like a class mosaic project and sand painting.

Throughout the month experiment with such varied projects as printmaking, papier-mâché, weaving, and texture collages.

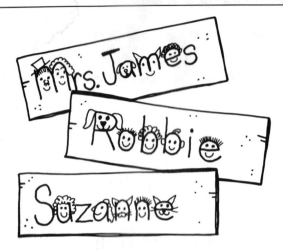

Names and Faces

Use name tags in a combination reading and art lesson. First, identify all the round letters. Then, in all these round areas the children draw faces or animals to depict family members and pets. Use as a colorful desk hanging for the beginning of the year.　Belle Bleifeld

Class Friendship Wreath

Give children small pieces of brightly colored construction paper to trace one hand on. Children cut out their hands, then help you arrange them in a circle to form the friendship wreath. Glue together, mount on cardboard, and hang.　May Kassicieh

Eye-Openers

Start the year with an adventure in optics by having students create pictures that will look three-dimensional when viewed through special glasses.

First, have children draw bold but simple designs on paper, like that illustrated above. Ask children to use primarily red and green in their drawings, as those colors produce the strongest three-dimensional effect. Make a pattern from paper for the glasses. Each child can use the pattern to cut two frames from lightweight cardboard. Sandwich one red and one green cellophane lens between each set of frames; glue pieces together and decorate as desired.

When most children look at their picture through the glasses, some lines will jump out and look three-dimensional. Tell pupils that the principle of "stereoscopic vision" or depth perception explains why this happens. For a detailed explanation, ask an optometrist to visit your class.　Sister Gwen Floryance

Name Tags That Last

Cut a piece of stiff oak tag into long strips. Measure the strips to fit each child, and have children use a marking pen to letter names on the front of each headband. Students can decorate headbands with crayons and staple when finished. The children love to wear them, and you'll love the way they last.

Thomas Bernagozzi

Birthday Flag

Fly a birthday flag when there is a class birthday. Cut the flag shape from an old, heavy cotton sheet. Hem the edges, then paint a birthday cake and the greeting "Happy Birthday." Use a staple gun to attach the banner to a discarded broom or mop handle. The birthday child holds the flag while the class sings to him or her.

Ellen Javernick

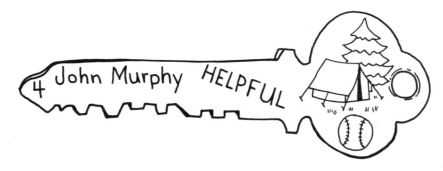

Keys to a Good Beginning

Start the year by helping upper graders think positively about themselves and their class. On the first day of school, give each student a sheet of heavy paper and a large key shape. Each traces around the shape, cuts it out, and decorates the key with five items of get-acquainted information: name, number of people in family, how he or she spent the summer vacation, a hobby, and one word telling something positive about him- or herself. Students take turns holding up their keys and sharing the information. At the end of the session, ask children if they can remember one fact about each of their classmates. This fosters memory, good attitudes about people, and class unity. The keys are then put on a bulletin board entitled "You Are the Key to a Good Classroom" for a week.

Jane Williams

Add-a-Month Train

The long, narrow shape of a train makes it ideal for a bulletin-board or wall decoration. Individual cars may be cut from construction paper, crayoned very large on a sheet of manila, or, for a 3-D project, made from milk cartons.

Each car might be a month piled with appropriate holiday and seasonal symbols. Or, each child can make a get-acquainted car with his or her name that contains pictures of hobbies and interest.

A Book About Me

Mother's or Father's Day is a long way off, but this gift for the occasion should be started now and added to through the year. Include pages showing now and end-of-the-year comparisons: heights and weights, self-portraits, likes and dislikes, and artwork.

On other pages, include outlines of the child's hands and feet; a picture of his or her house with full name, address, and telephone number; a drawing of family and pets; and a page showing certain skills acquired. At gift-giving time make a construction-paper cover, add the child's photo, and have him or her print his or her name.   Ellen Payzant

Magazine Collage

After discussing vacation activities, children search through discarded magazines for scenes, characters, and textures they can use to depict a summer experience. Students cut out and glue materials onto paper, then mount on construction paper.

Sister Gwen Floryance

Stenciled Desk Hanging

Have children use stencils to trace their name 10 times in two contrasting colors. Cut out and mount as shown. Add one brightly colored name to the top for a beginning-of-the-year desk hanging. Sister Gwen Floryance

Plaster Project

Ask each child to bring in a small plastic bag of natural items he or she has collected over the summer, such as sea shells, rocks, leaves, dried flowers, etc. Give each child a plastic foam bowl filled with one cup of patch plaster and 1/3 cup of sand. The children mix the sand and plaster with a plastic spoon while you pour in one cup of water. They should stir the mixture until it looks like Cream of Wheat. Once the plaster is mixed, students can stick their nature objects into the top of the plaster. While the plaster is still wet, sprinkle dry sand on top of it. Let dry. This item makes a nice paperweight. Christie Costanzo

Soft Self-Portraits

Students use box cardboard for backgrounds of full-figure self-portraits in favorite back-to-school outfits. Cut cardboard circles for backing heads, and rectangles or triangles for bodies. Cover circle with batting. Then pull a larger circle cut from the top part (less likely to run) of old panty hose over batting to back and tie with thread. Make features with yarn, sewing right through cardboard, batting, and nylon. Sew tubes of pantyhose fabric, and stuff for arms and legs. Cover body shapes with scraps of cloth to represent clothing. Glue all parts to background.
Helen Brown

School-Supply Design

Choose a single school supply or a combination—scissors, a ruler, a crayon, a paper clip, an eraser. Using a pencil, trace around the item on white paper. Overlap the first tracing and repeat. Color in the small sections created by the procedure. Sister Gwen Floryance

Chair Covers

Children can design and make simple slipcovers for backs of classroom chairs. Use them to honor birthdays or special accomplishments or to indicate classroom jobs.

Cut covers from oilcoth, fabric, tagboard, or plastic (from discarded shower curtains or tablecloths). Tape or sew sides together. Add decoration with paint, crayon, marker, colored tape, or adhesive-backed paper.

Face Designs

Cut an oval out of construction paper. Paste onto a contrasting color of construction paper, puffing slightly by stuffing tissue paper under the oval. Create facial features and costume with construction paper, yarn, and bits of fabric. Students may want to create self-portraits. Add names to the faces and use as back-to-school decorations. Joan Mary Macey

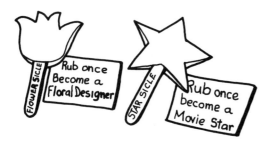

Wish-sicles

Cut out pairs of shapes to represent unfulfilled wishes. Use crayons to add details. Put a wooden Popsicle stick between the shapes and glue together. Label the stick ("Star-sicle"); on a small piece of paper write directions for use ("Rub once—become a movie star"). Put directions and Wish-sicles in individual envelopes. Let students share to help get acquainted.

Birthday Swingers

String a rope along a wall or across the ceiling. Have children write their names and birth dates on large shapes and attach to the rope. Try an apple for September, pumpkin for October, and so on. Summer birthdays can go after June birthdays.   Winifred Miller

Painting Seasons

This project is appropriate for children at all grade levels and provides a good back-to-school bridge. Divide a large sheet of oak tag into four equal sections. Label in pencil: fall, winter, spring, and summer. Discuss the different feelings of the seasons: the colors, moods, temperatures students feel when they think of that time of year.

Talk about the concept of abstract representation: that children will not be painting a picture to represent that season but will be using brushstrokes and colors to evoke the special mood. Give children time to plan their sections and time later to share their work.

Marla Kantor

Nature Prints

Arrange two or three weeds on newspaper and coat their surfaces with tempera. Move weeds to a base paper, place a cover sheet on top, and press firmly. Remove top sheet and allow your print to dry.

Susan P. Rapp

Jigsaw-Puzzle Art

Have children draw a large picture animal on oak tag. Cut it into puzzlelike sections. Trace each section onto a different material, such as textured paper, cardboard, or fabric. Mount each piece and assemble animal as a whole.

Sister Gwen Floryance

Paper Playgrounds

You will need a 4- by 6-inch sheet of white tagboard for each child, multicolored strips and scraps of construction paper, colored string, scissors, and white glue.

Put out piles of colored strips, paper scraps, and colored string. Tell the children that they will use the materials you have set out to design playground equipment for very tiny people. Demonstrate how to begin by selecting a colored strip, folding back one end about 1/2 inch, and pasting the end down on a tagboard sheet. Loop, twist, or fold the strip before pasting down the other end. Add another strip to create something like the illustration shown here. Now have each child take just five strips at first. After they've worked with these pieces, they can pick up more strips, scraps of paper, or string. Glue the ends of strips firmly to each other or to the base.

As children are finishing, you may ask them to show and tell us how they play or do tricks on the equipment they have designed.

Janet Carson

- *See page 70 for information on other art activities to help children communicate.*

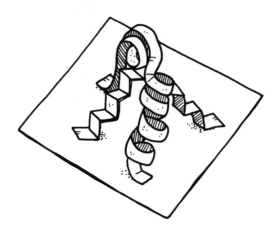

Mosaic Pictures

Paint heavy cardboard or light plywood for mosaic base. Sketch simple design, then use white glue to fill in each part with seeds, rice, corn, beans, and so on.

Armand Matte

Bookmarks with Personality

Have students make friendly bookmarks using small wooden spoons, plastic movable eyes found in craft stores, and scraps of paper and fake fur. Glue the fur on top of the wide end of the spoon. Glue on eyes, draw on a mouth, and add a bow tie, ribbon, or necklace.

Susan Thompson

One-Person Puppet Stage

Divide an 18-inch by 12-inch piece of heavy cardboard into three sections. Each end section should be 5 inches wide, leaving an 8-inch span in the center. Fold one end up, the other end down. Cut a 4-inch by 7-inch opening in the center section. Cut two 20-inch lengths of heavy string, knot them, put through holes in the center and in one end section, then tie together. Students wear stages as they perform with finger or hand puppets.

Belle Bleifeld

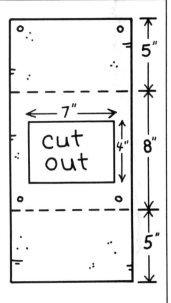

5"

7"

cut out

4"

8"

5"

Paper-Plate Swan

Swan's body is made from one plate cut in half. Cut neck and tail from double-weight rims and insert between two plate halves before gluing halves together. Scallop and cut apart fluted plate rims for feathers, and glue these on body. Glue swan to a black ground; add paper-scrap reeds to indicate the shoreline.

Friendly-Names Design

Have students use varied sizes of black construction paper, folded in half, on which to print the names of friends. Make sure many of the letters touch the fold. Carefully cut out each name, open, and paste onto contrasting poster board to create an interesting design.   Jay Scott

Community Helpers

Children often find it fun to design people from basic construction-paper shapes. Community helpers offer good subjects for this project as their clothing is distinctive and easily recognized.

For young children, some shapes (such as circle faces) can be precut. Older groups can use round jar lids and plates to aid in cutting even circles. Urge children to keep drawn or painted detail to a minimum, so completed figures will appear uncluttered.

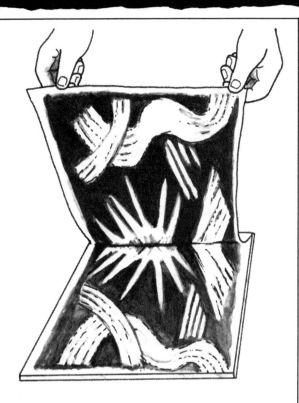

Prints With Pizzazz

Here's a fall printmaking project that's fast, fun, and easy to do. First, assemble the following equipment: several ink rollers, water-base printing ink or fingerpaint, inking slabs (metal or hard plastic sheets with edges taped for safety), white and/or colored construction paper, and drawing tools (cardboard strips, ice-cream sticks, toothbrushes, forks, etc.).

First, roll ink smoothly over the entire surface of the inking slab, then use a scrap of cardboard or other drawing tool to draw swirls and zigzags in the ink. Working quickly before the ink becomes dry, place a sheet of paper over the printing plate and press down. Remind students that the final product will be reversed. This is especially important when drawing words or letters. Add other colors for contrast when prints are dry.

Paula Guhin

Perky Penguins

First, cut a 10-inch penguin body from black construction paper and two 7-inch tear-shaped fins. Cut a bib from white paper and glue to front of body. Add white construction paper eyes. From orange construction paper, cut out flipper feet and a 2-inch square, folded diagonally, to make a beak. Bend feet up and fins back to make the penguin stand. Send home notes to parents or student work in penguin's beak.

Newfield School Kindergarten Teachers

Dot Drawing

Instead of drawing by lines, have students draw with dots. Use permanent black markers or permanent black ink. Children can create little whimsical shapes, hidden letters or symbols, flowers, starfish, balloons, butterflies, etc. Fill in the designs with watercolor paints.

Susan Major Tingey

Bird Feeder

Using flour and water paste, students glue seeds that birds like in a design in a shoebox lid. Staple a loop of twine to the top of the lid to hang bird feeder.   Ruth Ann Johnson

Pinch a Pot

Make a simple pot more interesting by giving it an animal shape. Have children take a piece of clay about the size of an orange and use their thumbs to "pinch" a pot with smooth, thick walls. Pull out feet for the vessel to stand on and don't forget a tail! The head can be pulled from the clay or securely attached later. Faces can be painted on with bright colors.   Marla Kantor

• *See page 70 for a clay resource kit.*

Stained-Glass Window

Fold a square piece of black construction paper in quarters. Draw a line about an inch thick on the two outside open edges for a frame. Draw and cut out floral shapes. Leave spaces of black between cuts. Don't cut into space reserved for frame.

Open the paper and attach to the sticky side of clear contact paper. Fill in cut-out areas with colored tissue paper or cellophane. Place a piece of contact paper on the back to enclose, and you have a stained-glass window.

Susan Major Tingey

Magazine Op-Art

Save those magazines! Have students decide how to cut an appealing picture. The same geometrical shape cut again and again works well. Lightly sketch guidelines for cutting onto the picture. Cut and mount on complementary colored paper.   Sister Gwen Floryance

Paper-Cup Hand Puppets

Turn a paper cup upside down and add features with paint or cut paper. If the cup has a handle, use it for holding and manipulating, or turn it around and make it the nose of your puppet.

Dinosaur Mural

Your class can create a giant mural without standing at a wall vying for elbowroom. Draw a dinosaur scene on a continuous sheet of roll paper, first in pencil, then traced with a black marker. Divide the mural into squares using a pencil, according to the number of children involved in the project. Make color slash marks to indicate what color a section should be. Large areas to be cut in two will need color slash marks on either side of the cut line. Cut mural along pencil lines, labeling each piece on back with a number and letter for placement later (i.e., A-1 in top left).

Children color diagonally, from upper right to lower left, to make pieces blend together. Once squares are completed, tape together on the wall. This activity is also a lesson in cooperation. Children learn how, by working as a team, they can accomplish something that would be difficult to do individually.

Christie Costanzo

Kachina Dolls

Each winter, the Hopi of the Southwest have a ceremony to dedicate their services to spirits, or Kachinas, in return for a good harvest. Kachina dolls are crafted for children to play with so that they will learn to recognize the real Kachinas.

Using pictures of authentic Kachina dolls as guides, students can create their own original dolls. Materials needed include cardboard tubes, glue, and an assortment of paper, yarn, pipe cleaners, felt, toothpicks, and so on.

Gretchen Treitz and Thaïs Kaufman Wright

Native American Mosaic

Try this giant wall mosaic that has Native American flair. First, sketch a design on a large piece of paper. Using different colored markers, indicate what color each section should be. Divide the paper into sections, one for each student. Number the sections on the back of the paper, then cut them apart. Cut colored construction paper into half-inch squares. Have each child glue the squares onto his or her section of the mosaic. Tape the sections together and presto—a magnificent mosaic! Christie Costanzo

- *Observe Native American Day by making one of these projects. See page 70 for reference materials on Native American crafts.*

Sioux Shields

The Plains Indians, who include the Arapaho, the Osage, and the Sioux, were buffalo hunters. They used dried buffalo hide to make ceremonial shields that were believed to provide magical as well as physical protection. The shields; designs, which often radiate out from the center, were said to come to their owners in a dream.

To make their own special shields, students begin by soaking large brown grocery bags in warm water to unseal the glue. Wring out the excess water and crumple the paper into a ball to create wrinkles. Then uncrumple the paper and lay it out to dry. Cut large circles from the textured paper.

Now instruct students to fold the circle in half twice to form equal quarters. Students should paint a Native American symbol in the shield's center, using pictures of real shields for inspiration. Next, have them draw another shape in one quarter and then repeat it in the other three in the same location. This is done several times until the shield is filled and a radiating design becomes apparent. Finished shields can be mounted on cardboard to make them stiff.

Gretchen Treitz and Thaïs Kaufman Wright

Buffalo Hide

Celebrate Native American Day by making and decorating "buffalo hides." Students place large, brown paper bags on their desks with the bottoms facing the ceiling and the seam side facing them. They cut along the seam toward the bottom and cut along bottom edges until it is separated from the rest of the bag. Discard the bottom. One long piece remains. Tear edges for an uneven look. Students colorfully illustrate a Native American story on hides. Next, glue four strips of wood or cardboard together at the corners to make a frame.

After randomly punching holes around the hide edges, measure two arm lengths of yarn. Tie one end to frame near first hole to be sewn. Wrap cellophane or masking tape to other end of the yarn to facilitate sewing.

Sew in an under-over-under-over fashion through hide holes and around frame.

Gail Neu

• *See page 70 for reference materials on Native American crafts.*

Navajo Sand Paintings

The Navajo of northern New Mexico and Arizona are noted for their spectacular sand paintings.

Students will enjoy making their own sand paintings. You'll need crayons, sandpaper, white glue, paint brushes, and colored sand. (Inexpensive aquarium sand is available at pet stores.)

First, show examples of Native American art. Next, give each student a piece of sandpaper and have him or her use crayons to draw a geometrical design, using patterns similar to those created by the Navajo. Students can create symmetrical paintings by folding their sandpaper in half, drawing a design on one side and then mirroring it on the other. Or, students may paint a message, using picture symbols for others to decipher.

After the drawings are completed, have students use a paintbrush to cover selected areas of their design with glue. Then dust colored sand over the glue and shake off the excess. So that the sand colors do not mix, glue only one color of sand at a time, allowing each color to dry before adding the next.

Gretchen Treitz and Thaïs Kaufman Wright

• *See page 70 for reference materials on Native American crafts.*

Pueblo Pottery

The Pueblo women of the Southwest have been making beautiful pottery for 1,500 years. Most pottery was made by the coil method—pieces of clay rolled into slender lengths and built one atop the other in a spiral—but primary students can easily attempt the less delicate Pueblo "pinch pots." Self-hardening clay, water, and a variety of engraving tools (forks, nails, pencils, and so on) are all that's needed. To make a pinch pot, students should roll a small handful of clay into a ball. Then insert a thumb into the center of the clay and rotate the ball, pressing thumb to fingers against the clay to "open" the pot. Water can be applied to smooth the clay. When students are pleased with the shape of their pots, they can use different tools to create a textured surface. Let pots dry, then have students paint them.

Gretchen Treitz and Thaïs Kaufman Wright

Papier-Mâché Plates

Cover an 8-inch plastic foam plate with 2-inch strips of torn or cut newsprint dipped in a thin mixture of flour and water. When dry, separate the papier-mâché from the plastic foam mold. There are a variety of techniques for adding color, including splatter painting, sponge painting, and spray painting.

Christie Costanzo

Sock Hand Puppets

Put a sock on your hand with the heel where your wrist bends. For ears, cut two V-shaped slits near the heel at each side and poke up to the desired angle. Cover the openings made by the cuts with a wig or hat. If you have a friend with big feet, ask for a sock. When the outer edges of the foot section are folded back and sewn, you have an elephant, complete with trunk.

Canned Characters

Mr. Green Beans and Ms. Orange Blossom emerge from empty cans. (Use nonmetal cans with very young children.) Let label of can suggest a character. Glue together a paper tube that fits inside the can and is 3 or 4 inches taller. Glue head, arms, legs, and clothing cut from colored paper, pieces of advertisements, or another can label onto this tube. Add facial features and yarn hair.

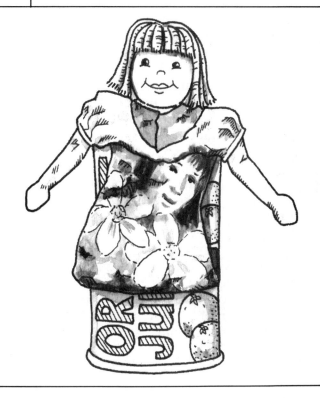

Flip-Over Games

Make pocket games from the plastic bubbles used to package notions. For a two-in-one game, use matching bubbles and two pairs of beads. Trace around bubble and cut cardboard. Think of two designs using beads as elements (eyes, spots, wheels, and buttons). Punch holes where beads should go. Draw one design on front, one on back of cardboard. Put beads under bubbles and glue edges down. Tilt the game and try to roll the beads into the holes!

Pooh Puppets

Make Winnie the Pooh characters come alive with this project! Wad a double sheet of newspaper into a softball-sized ball and secure with strips of masking tape. Cut tagboard strips 3 by 3 inches. Roll into a tube to fit over an empty soda bottle neck and secure with masking tape. Insert the tagboard tube deep into the newspaper ball and secure with more masking tape. Put the puppet head ball and tube onto the bottle neck. If odd-shaped features are needed (long ears for Eeyore, a beak for Owl, a snout for Piglet), tape strips of thick newspaper to the appropriate spot.

Next, tear school paper towels into strips an inch wide. Mix up several containers of wheat paste and water and stir by hand until moderately thick and smooth.

Students dip a piece of paper towel into the paste, remove excess with two fingers, and smoothly place the strip of paper over the newspaper ball. They repeat the process until the entire ball and special head parts are covered.

Leave puppet heads to dry overnight. Students paint them with tempera paint the next day. When the base is dry, students add facial features.

When the painting is completed and dry, students can add a simple body suit, gluing it to the tagboard cone, which is the neck. The suit should be large enough for a student's hand. Costumes can be made from pieces of scrap material. Fingers are inserted in the neck tube to control the head.

Phyllis J. Perry

Line Drawing

Call students' attention to the space inside what is being drawn. Have children divide this space into shaped areas with a light pencil line. Then, using close-together parallel lines, fill in these areas. Suggest separating the spaces from each other by changing the position of the lines in each area; make them horizontal, vertical, or diagonal. Curving some of the lines will give more surface contour. Tracing over pencil lines with felt pens will heighten the effect.

Curler Creatures

Discarded plastic, foam, or mesh hair rollers can be wound with odds and ends of yarn, then glued or sewn together to make amusing animals. Use a large-eyed blunt needle for sewing; heavy craft glue for gluing. Pin mesh or foam curlers in place while gluing. Colored paper and pipe cleaners are good for adding details. Rollers may also be taped or wired together, then covered with papier-mâché and painted.

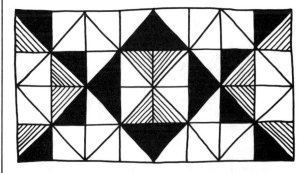

Paper Quilts

Fold, then unfold, a sheet of plain white paper to create a pattern of geometric shapes. Paint the shapes in a symmetrical fashion to produce a colorful quiltlike pattern. Dry, then crumple paper into a ball to achieve a puckered texture. Press out and mount on construction paper. Jacqueline Koury

- *See page 70 for fiction and nonfiction books about quilting.*

Paper Herd

Trace an animal pattern onto different-colored sheets of tissue paper and cut out. Glue pieces to white paper, then trim as shown. Mount on construction paper.

Sister Gwen Floryance

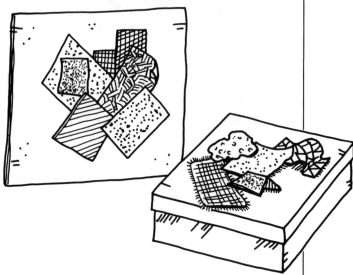

Sandpaper Art

Working with sandpaper can help young children develop an awareness of various textures.

Have available a supply of sandpaper ranging in texture from very fine to coarse. After the children feel the various sheets of sandpaper, ask them to describe how the textures differ. Have them contrast the very rough quality of the sandpaper with the texture of some pieces of smooth-surfaced classroom furniture made of varnished or laminated woods, or of rigid plastic.

Suggest that the children make sandpaper collages by cutting abstract shapes from sandpaper and pasting them on dark-colored construction paper.

Or make multitexture collages by incorporating abstract shapes of sandpaper, nylon net, corduroy, burlap, denim, synthetic sponge, wool tweed, cotton lace, and so on. Each collage might be glued to the lid of an empty gift box and taken home. Such boxes are perfect for storing children's personal trinkets and treasures.

Paper-Plate Clown Puppet

This clown face is also a puppet head. Glue plates rim to rim after cutting a hand hold in back plate. Add hair and features made from yarn or paper scraps.

Stained-Glass Surprise

With a black permanent marker, draw a bold design on manila paper. Color in with colored markers. Coat both sides of paper with cooking oil by dabbing on with tissue. Blot off excess oil, frame, and hang in a sunny window.

Pamela Klawitter

Fairy-Tale Puppets

Here's a fun storytelling puppet to make for younger children. You'll need an empty $4\frac{1}{4}$-by-$4\frac{1}{4}$-by-$5\frac{1}{2}$-inch tissue box, sheets of construction paper, a variety of pasta shapes, buttons, fabric scraps, and felt-tip markers. First, choose a specific fairy tale, such as "Goldilocks and the Three Bears," and make cutout characters to illustrate the story. Paint the tissue box and turn it upside down so that the opening is facing the bottom. Then attach the characters to each side of the box. Delight students by sticking your hand inside the hole at the bottom and turning the box as you tell the fairy tale. You may also wish to attach pieces of Velcro to the box and to the characters so that you can easily change cutouts and tell other stories. Sheri L. Dressler

Wacky Weaving

Construction-paper weaving takes a new twist with this playful loom-design project. Start by making a standard straight-cut loom from contrasting strips of construction paper. Then weave thin strips of a third color through the loom and glue on paper-punch circles, squiggles, and spirals to add interest. Encourage students to elaborate on the straight-cut loom design by making wavy and zigzag patterns. Finished weavings make wonderful wall displays.

Pamela Klawitter

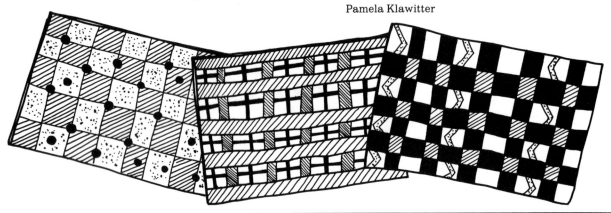

Stained-Glass Rubbings

To do a rubbing of any kind is to instantly understand the meaning of texture. One of the most effective objects to use for rubbing is, believe it or not, a plastic doily. For a unique treatment, place black paper on the doily and rub the surface with the side of a metallic crayon. Fill in some of the completed rubbing with a heavy colored crayon or oil pastel. This gives a rich, stain-glass look. Try cutting around the rubbing and mounting it on a contrasting background.

Ireene Robbins

Rope Creatures

Cut sisal rope into 12-inch and 15-inch lengths. Soak in water for a couple of minutes. Have children decide what creature they'd like to make and experiment tying knots for the head, feet, and so on. For special effects, use knots of different sizes, or unravel parts of the rope.

Doris D. Breiholz

OCTOBER

   Leaf rubbings, sun catchers, and shadow boxes are only some of the nature crafts that celebrate fall this month.

   At Halloween, things are seldom what they seem. Paper plates, pine cones, milk cartons, and other easy-to-find materials masquerade as noise-makers, mobiles, and masks. Expect the unexpected in Halloween projects!

Dye-Dip Leaves

Invite children to create this display with leaves they made from paper coffee filters and food coloring. Children fold filters, then dip edges into different colors of the diluted dye. Press between paper toweling, then cut into leaf shapes and arrange on a door or window for a "Welcome Fall" display.

Angela Andrews

Fall Scene

Bring autumn's colors into your classroom with leaves students collect during a nature walk. To preserve leaves, wipe them with cooking oil and press between sheets of newspaper. When dry, attach to a construction-paper fall scene for the bulletin board.

Laurie Schwartzer

Milkweed Pod Shadow Boxes

Paint milkweed pods or leave plain. Coat the insides with glue and attach small weeds, tiny dried flowers, seeds, artificial greens, and so on. Make hanging loops with needle and gold thread.

Elaine Scarpino

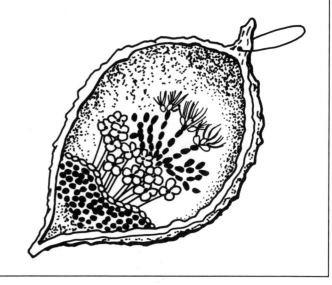

Eraser-Blended Leaves

To make realistically shaded leaves, draw the light outline of a simple leaf and crayon a heavy line of color around the inside of this outline. With the eraser end of a pencil, push this crayoned color toward the center of the leaf shape. A suggestion of leaf veins may be made with pencil or ink lines. Completed leaves may be cut out and used to form a colorful border for bulletin boards or glued in pleasing designs onto place mats, book covers, or decorative boxes.

Fall Reflections

Fold a sheet of paper in half. Paint watercolor trees on the top half, intermittently refolding to create "reflections." Add details to upper trees. Apply a wash to the bottom half, using few strokes to avoid muddying the colors.   Susan Major Tingey

Leaf Sun Catcher

Press a leaf under books until flat and dry. Place the dried leaf between two pieces of plastic wrap. Cut two identical leaf-shaped frames from construction paper and glue to each side of the plastic. Trim the plastic, add a thread hanger, and display.   Jay Scott

Podscapes

Draw an autumn scene on a sheet of construction paper. Fill in the design with different kinds of seeds or pods, gluing pods to paper. Add details with markers or crayons.

Jay Scott

Nature Plaques

Use the real and unreal together in an autumn-inspired plaque. On the back of a paper plate, paint the shape of a particular tree. Attach a leaf of the tree and seed (such as an acorn) if available. Wax or press leaf first. Then attach with a folded-paper spring to make it appear to float away from the background. Glue on additional foliage in autumn colors of tissue or construction paper cut into little squares. Cover plate with cellophane wrap and add a cut-paper frame.

Falling Leaves

Paint the backs of real autumn leaves with neutral-colored acrylic paint. Press the leaves against a white piece of paper to make prints. When the paint is dry, paint prints lightly with watercolors. Cut out leaf prints. Glue to a piece of blue construction paper to look like the sky. Lightly draw clouds with chalk or white-colored pencil.

Susan Major Tingey

Fall Shadow Boxes

Cover box lid with colored paper. Cover cardboard strips as wide as the lid is deep with the same paper and glue in the box to section it off. Glue contrasting paper in each section for background. Arrange such fall findings as nuts, pods, weeds, leaves, and so on.

Jeremy Tyler

Leaf Prints

Start collecting light-colored, solid, and printed cloth. Cut into 9-by 9-inch squares. Have students collect leaves. Dip a paintbrush into acrylic paint and carefully paint over each leaf. Turn leaf over onto material. Cover with paper, press, and print!

Vlasta Krieger

Textured Trees

To capture the texture and rustle of fall leaves, snip bright tissue paper into confetti-size bits. Attach to paper by dropping the paper bits onto areas of wet glue. Combine with other media to create colorful autumn scenes.

Younger children might make a single tree, cutting the trunk from wrinkled brown paper or a scrap of brown fabric. Older groups may prefer to do action pictures of fall activities, combining painted or crayoned sections with tissue bits.

Leaf Rubbings

Mount pictures of several different kinds of leaves on tagboard. Follow the outline and leaf veins with a thin ribbon of white glue. Let dry overnight. Fasten pastel colors of duplicating paper to the tagboard with paper clips. Gently rub the side of a crayon, or several crayons, over the leaf patterns to simulate the varying shades of fall leaves.

Aileen M. LeBlanc

Autumn Nature Crafts

If your art budget is low, these craft ideas will see you through the fall with some scraps and a few bottles of glue. Assign students to comb their yards, the playground, etc. for seed pods, pine cones, burrs, leaves, berries, nuts, and the like.

Make a squirrel by gluing an acorn for a head onto a pine cone for the body. Add brown felt ears and tiny beads for the eyes and nose. Use paint and markers to finish the features. Brown pipe cleaners serve as its hands and feet. Cut and glue on a piece of brown felt for a tail. Perch it atop a walnut half.

Make a floral picture using seeds, berries, and other materials to form the flowers. Glue them onto a construction paper mat for display.

Mary MacDonald

Rub and Crinkle

Here's a new twist to the familiar art of leaf rubbing. Gather leaves of different sizes and shapes. Children arrange several in a pleasing pattern, then place a sheet of newsprint paper over the leaves. Rub crayons back and forth on the paper until each leaf appears. Encourage children to use several colors of crayon, rubbing over each leaf more than once. When each paper is filled with rubbings, have the child crumple it into a ball, then dip it in a container of cold-water dye or watercolor paint. (Reminder: Wear rubber gloves when working with cold-water dye.) Uncrumple the rubbing and lay it flat on newspaper to dry. You'll find the dye will be darker where there are "crinkle wrinkles." Finish by cutting the dyed paper into a large leaf shape, if desired. When laminated, these dyed rubbings make beautiful place mats.   Marla Kantor

Fall Silhouette

Rule a margin around black paper. Draw a tree, branches touching margin. Cut out. On white paper, glue a scene made from torn colored paper. Glue tree to background.   Sister Gwen Floryance

Leaf Overlay

Place a piece of red, green, yellow, or orange tissue paper over a leaf (vein side up) and rub with a peeled crayon. Tear out rubbings and arrange on manila paper. Mix one part white glue to four parts water and carefully "paint" over the leaves. Brush out the colors to blend with each other all the way to the edge of the paper. Vlasta Krieger

Columbus Day Plate

Using large paper plates, children can create simple and bold impressions of the Nina, Pinta, and Santa Maria. The entire design may be torn from contrasting shades of colored paper and pasted to a rubbed pastel background. Special textured effects, such as toothpick masts, billowing paper-handkerchief sails, yarn rigging, and cotton foam-tipped waves, may be added. Try different arrangements before the final pasting.

- *See page 70 for books that help set the scene for Columbus Day.*

Columbus's Ships

These ships are easy to put in a bottle when you use paper, colored markers, and plastic wrap. Have students cut paper in a bottle shape. Draw one large ship or three small ones on paper; cut out and glue on the bottle. Cover with plastic wrap for glass effect; tape wrap to back of bottle to secure.

Joan Mary Macey

Bottled Boats

Celebrate Columbus Day with this bottled boats project. Have each child draw a bottle outline on light blue construction paper. Draw bottle caps with black crayons or felt-tipped pens. After researching various types of sailing vessels, each child draws an authentic model inside the outline of the bottle. Children can paste a few tufts of cotton along the bottoms of boats to show foaming waves. Finally, have them cut around their bottle outlines and cover the creations with clear plastic wrap.

Jane K. Priewe

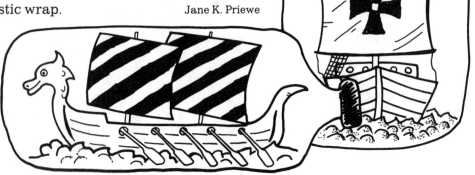

Fire Prevention Friend

Children can create a friendly fire fighter from a bathroom-tissue roll decorated with colored paper, crayons, and glue-ons. Supply metallic paper or foil for shiny badge and ax.

When figures are done, discuss items to be put on a home fire-safety checklist, such as improperly stored painting supplies and defective chimneys.

Completed individual lists might be rolled up and placed inside the little figures to take home.

- *This is a good project for National Fire Prevention Week.*

Lunch Trays

In honor of National School Lunch Week discuss the four food groups. Then, with a variety of materials, create artistic examples of balanced meals. Sister Gwen Floryance

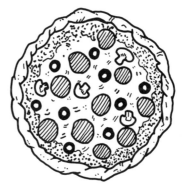

Pizza With Everything

Frozen crusts and some complete pizzas are packaged on large plastic-foam circles. Cover circle with brown paper toweling soaked in wallpaper paste. Twist a ropelike piece for edge of "crust." Dry, then paint center red. Let paint dry and brush on thinned white glue. Sprinkle with sawdust. Add favorite "extras" from construction paper.

Nancy Wimmer

- *This project, too, ties in well with National School Lunch Week. Or, celebrate Pizza Festival Time!*

Paper in Motion

You will need tissue paper in 10 colors cut into 3- by 5-inch pieces (one of each color per child), white drawing paper, manila paper cut in 3- by 5-inch rectangles, watercolor brushes, scissors, and white glue.

Begin by asking these questions: Did you ever see photographs of athletes in motion that show overlapping views of the action? You are going to show action using overlapped pieces of colored tissue paper. Who can name some good action subjects for the pictures? What runs? hops? swims? flies? Then have each student draw just the outline of the object he or she has chosen on a manila rectangle, then cut out the silhouette and trace it onto one of the sheets of colored tissue. Place the other nine sheets underneath and carefully cut through all 10 layers at once. (Tell students to cut slowly and keep a firm grasp, turning the paper as they cut.) Discard the manila stencils. Next, each child will need to decide how to arrange the pieces. They can be overlapped in a sweeping arc, on a diagonal (like a diver), or in an up-and-down fashion (like a hopping rabbit). Chil-

dren should make their choice based on what would be a natural movement for their object.

Encourage children to be sensitive to the colors that are blended as the tissue silhouettes are overlapped. When they feel they have an appealing arrangement, they can glue the tissues in place on the white drawing paper.

As students are finishing, ask: How did you come up with this object? Have you ever seen a real one in motion? Is the sense of movement greater when looking at the picture from a distance or close up?

Janet Carson

- *See page 70 for information on other art activities to help children communicate.*

Sweet and Sour Apples

Children love to "make faces." Let them cut two identical circles and draw a sad face on one and a happy face on the other. Glue circles together, back to back. Then add color and other features to create a special character or object. Possibilities are many: suns, clowns, jack-o'-lanterns, puppies, and other animals.

The finished double personalities can be used as daily weather recorders or to indicate when children complete certain goals or projects.

- *Celebrate National Apple Month with this project!*

Halloween Houses

Begin the project by having the class research architectural terms associated with the traditional Victorian haunted house: arched windows, double-hung Gothic plank doors, gables, dormers, cupolas, gingerbread, and balustrades.

Now have students include some of these features in their haunted houses. Have each do an initial sketch on plain paper before transferring the final sketch to construction paper. Have children cut out their houses; then, using craft knives or single-edge razor blades and working on a padded surface, cut around three sides of doors and windows so they will open and close. (Supervise this step closely.) Paste scraps of paper behind the openings, then glue creatures on the paper to peek behind windows and doors. Have students make realistic trees to place around their houses, sketching first before drawing on construction paper. Glue each house and trees to a large sheet of paper.

For a spine-tingling display, mount several houses and trees together beneath a shakily lettered invitation: Visit our neighborhood—if you dare!

Jeanne Swintkowski

Twirling Cats

Have each child draw and cut a cat's head and body freehand. Encourage everyone to think big. Add green or yellow eyes and a tail cut spiral fashion from a paper circle. Suspend cats from different lengths of string.

Sally Stempinski

Spooky Spider

Draw a web on paper. Glue yarn to web. Cut out a spider body and legs. Staple folded legs under body. Paste cotton on body. Attach to web.

Sister Gwen Floryance

Halloween Fence

This Halloween fence is made by gluing together toilet tissue rolls, painting them dark gray, and attaching straight strips of cardboard, using brass fasteners. The fence sitters could be all sorts of Halloween creatures. Jacqueline Koury

Pumpkin People

Place orange crepe paper underneath clean milk cartons or juice containers, bring paper together at the top, and tie with a bow. Have children add black construction-paper features, and display your creatures. They make a fun motley crew to enjoy and take home.

Kathy Rocafuerte

Fat Cats

Mark a lunch bag into a head and body with black crayon. Students use black to outline features and colors for details. They add feet, tails, hats, then stuff and staple top shut. Perch on top of the Halloween fence. Carol Hutchison

Patchy Scarecrow

To make this jolly scarecrow you'll need four ice-cream sticks; a plastic container lid; sheets of construction paper; small, rectangular scraps of material; buttons; and yarn. First, make the scarecrow's body by gluing four ice-cream sticks together to form a "T," three vertically, one horizontally. For the head, cover the plastic lid with a construction-paper circle and glue it in place. Add buttons for eyes and a construction-paper nose and mouth. Cut a notch at the side of the lid and afix it to the top of the ice-cream-stick frame. Next, make a suit from brown construction paper; attach patches, buttons down the front, and yarn to the cuffs. To assemble the scarecrow, glue the suit to the frame. Let dry thoroughly.

Sally Jarvis

Wise Owl

Cut an owl from brown and tan construction paper. Make eyes from orange and yellow pieces of construction paper. Tear up small pieces of newspaper, and glue to chest area for a mottled feather look. Display as part of the Halloween decoration.

Weirdies

October is a month to excite imaginations. What better time to create goblins and monsters? Cut feet (or claws) from cardboard and attach to the bottom of a paper bag with a paper fastener. Stuff bag; tie at top. Style hairdos from fringed fabric, frayed rope, yarn, cut tissue, or crepe paper. Paint or paste on noses and other features. Tiny creatures may sit on desktops; larger relatives guard door.

Cave of Creepy Crawlies

Create a scary scene from paper, magazine cutouts, and imagination. Cut the outer opening of a cave from construction paper. Fill in interior with magazine photos or design own paper rocks and cave formations. Make creatures for inside and outside cave from yarn, fur, paper; cut others from magazine photos. Add trees and spider webs with black marker.

Kathleen Decker

Witch Mobile

Make this Halloween decoration with black, white, and red construction paper or felt. Cut out all the parts shown in the picture—two hats, warts, chins, mouths, and noses. Cut four eyeballs and eye backings. Paste the pairs together and string with black thread or yarn. Children might like to add special effects with glitter.

Jane K. Priewe

A Fistful of Ghosts

With a flick of the wrist, a handprint becomes a ghost. Make a paint pad from a folded, wet paper towel and white tempera paint. Press the little finger side of the hand onto the pad and then onto background paper with "a bit of a swish." The little finger makes the head, the bottom of the hand creates the ghost.

Becky Kaupelis

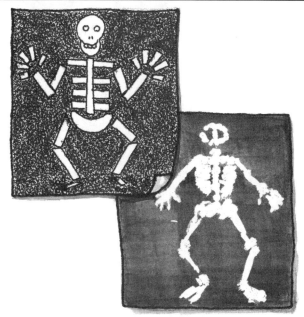

Wise Young Owl

For a true bird-in-the-round, use a cork float or Styrofoam ball for owl's body. Glue on a piece of construction paper shaped to form horned crest, wings, and feet. A narrow strip of brown wrapping paper, firmly twisted, makes a sturdy perch. Real or colored-paper leaves can be attached to the "branch."

Spooky Skeletons

Pencil a skeleton on black paper. Glue white straws to sketch. Add background. Color a white skeleton and scene on white paper. Cover with a black watercolor wash.

Sister Gwen Floryance and Jan Swift

Lunch-Bag Pumpkin

Use regular brown paper lunch bags to make this craft. Color the bottom half of the lunch bag orange and draw a jack-o'-lantern face on it. Color the top half of the bag green for the stem. Cut several vertical slits from the top of the bag to the edge of the orange part of the bag, about 1/2 inch apart. Cinch the green slits together with a green ribbon to create a stem.

James Perrin

Halloween Noisemaker

Staple edges of two plates after placing several small stones between them. Fasten to a dowel handle, and add whirling color by stapling paper circles to yarn fastened to the handle.

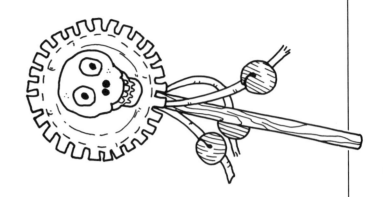

Mâché a Mask

Just in time for Halloween, each child in your class can create a mask. Use one blown-up balloon for every two children. Working in pairs, students cover the entire balloon with three layers of wet papier-mâché strips. Leave the tie exposed so that the balloon can be popped when dry.

After balloons are popped, cut the shell in two so each child has his or her own half to make into a mask. Cut eyes with scissors. Build additional features by scrunching up small pieces of dry newspaper and pasting them into shapes with wet strips. Allow the face to dry before decorating with tempera paint and exciting scraps.　Marla Kantor

• *See page 70 for resource books to inspire creative maskmaking.*

Paper-Plate Masks

Give each child a 9-inch-round paper plate with the center cut out. Each decorates the rim of the paper plate in any way he or she chooses. For instance, a witch's mask is easily made by gluing a large black triangle across the top of the plate to form a hat. Colored yarn or crepe paper can be added to make hair. Bits of fake fur pasted around the edge will become a cat or other animal. Add appropriate paper ears and whiskers. When the masks are decorated, simply attach elastic, string, or yarn as ties.　Virginia Ankeny

Bird Masks

Sketch mask on cardboard and cut out. Add a cardboard beak, topknot, and other features. Paint with a light watercolor wash, then accent with a darker wash. Highlight details or add patterns with markers. Festoon with streamers or feathers and glue colored cellophane behind eyes. Add a decorated stick handle.

Laura Revness and Michael Brozda

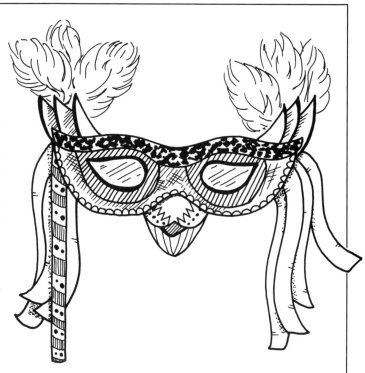

Spooky Tray Masks

The base of this mask is a frozen food dinner tray. Poke ample eyeholes and smaller ventilating holes. Have children conceal the contours of the tray by covering it with bulky yarn. (Don't cover the holes.) They should glue yarn in concentric patterns suggested by the shapes of the tray sections. Attach yarn ties at the sides of the masks.

James Perrin

Giant Masks

Cardboard shipping boxes are just what you'll need to save for this fun-filled project. While one child slips a box over his or her head, the partner marks where eyeholes should be. (Place the box on a table and help students cut out eyeholes.) Help students cut holes. Choose bright, contrasting colors; paint and decorate boxes, adding beaks, ears, and other fanciful trimmings. Decorated eyes should not fall where eyeholes do.

Jay Scott

Spooky Specs

Cut a pair of glasses from a piece of black 9-by-12-inch construction paper. Three pairs can be cut from one piece. Decorate spooky specs with ghosts cut from white construction paper. Glue ghosts over the nose piece and at sides of glasses by stems. For peekaboo glasses, glue a construction paper letter "B" on the left stem, an "O" and a ghost on the center stem, and the last "O" over the right stem. Wear them for a Halloween outlook!

L. E. Putnam

Spooky Cat

Cut two circles from a brown paper bag for the cat's head. Staple the circles together around the perimeter, leaving one-fourth of the circle unstapled. Insert crumpled paper between the circles for stuffing. Staple the rest of the circle closed. Cut two triangles from a paper bag and staple on the circle for ears. Paint the front and back of the cat black. Cut eyes, nose and mouth from white construction paper and apply with glue. Glue white pipe cleaners to cat's nose for whiskers. The pupil of the cat's eye is made with black construction paper.

Joan Mary Macey

Kachina Masks

After learning about the significance of kachina dolls or masks, draw kachina features on a large sheet of coarse sandpaper. Color with contrasting tempera paints, and outline features in black. Glue sandpaper sheet to same-size tagboard backing. Cut out mask, leaving narrow margins on top and sides as shown. Cut out eye and mouth holes. Punch holes in ears and attach yarn ties.

James Perrin

• *See page 70 for resource material on Native American crafts.*

Two Hoots

A ribbed-edge paper plate immediately suggests the round, feathered form of an owl. Paint the entire plate with brown tempera. (Add a little detergent to the paint if the plate has a highly glazed surface so it will adhere more readily.) Cut the horned crest and tail from colored paper. Paste these onto plate, along with the eyes, beak, and cottony throat. Make a smaller owl by using the rim of the plate to form tail and folded-over crest. Try fluted cupcake liners or candy papers for eyes.

Halloween Hang-Ups

Decorate your room with Halloween mobiles. Ask children to think of words that remind them of this spooky holiday. Cut the words out of construction paper and hang them from the ceiling with brightly colored yarn. Dorothy Zjawin

Canny Candy Holders

Tin cans are easily decorated with bands of colored paper and various glue-ons to represent Halloween personalities. Hat (or hair) should fit can top so it can be easily taken off for adding and removing candy treats.

Props add to the charm of these tin-can people. Make pumpkins from stuffed circles of orange tissue paper, held together at the top with a dab of glue and twists of green paper. Turn a tiny cork ball or bead into a cat by adding paper ears and tail.

Pumpkin Pockets

Cut two identical pumpkin shapes and pumpkin "lids" from orange construction paper. Cut out jack-o'-lantern faces on each of the pumpkins. Staple the edges of the pumpkins together, leaving the entire top portion unstapled. Cut pieces of black and yellow construction paper big enough to slip inside behind the jack-o'-lantern faces and glue them in place. The pumpkin will seem to be lit by candlelight when the yellow side is facing you. The black paper behind the face will make the pumpkin look as if the candle was blown out. Use a butterfly paper fastener to attach the lid to the pumpkin.

Roxann Hieb

Tear a Monster

Challenge pupils with this assignment: create a monster without looking. Tell each student to fold a sheet of paper in half vertically. Hold it behind his or her back and think where monster's head, arms, waist, and legs should be. Tear slowly to shape. Unfold the creation and make one last tear, then color.

Sister Gwen Floryance

Halloween How-w-w-lers

Have children use a black crayon and a sheet of newsprint. Without lifting their crayon, they can draw three ghostly figures, filling in facial features. (Open mouths and lips are the most effective.) Next, cut out ghosts (including eyes) and paint with eerie shades of blue, green, and purple watercolors. Mount each spooky mural on black paper. "Early finishers" can make moons and clouds.

Ellen Javernick

Pumpkin Noisemaker

Partially fill a small container with rice. Tape on a lid. Cover with orange paper. Wrap a small box in green paper; glue to container. Add features with pasta painted black. Attach a handle.

Jay Scott

Sensational Scarecrows

Your students will have a ball making autumn scarecrows to decorate the classroom. Have students cut body parts and clothing from colored construction paper and glue together. Glue straw on head for hair and around pant cuffs and sleeves for a more authentic look.

Cynthia Poteracki

Newsworthy Witch

Give several sheets of old newspaper to each child to use in cutting out a witch's hat, gown, shoes, and hands. Cut the face, hair, arms, and legs from scraps of construction paper of various colors. Paste all parts together. Draw features and other details with marker.

Annie Burns Hicks

Haunted Halloween Houses

For each house you'll need one small, brown paper bag; construction paper (orange, yellow, white, and black); crayons or markers; sheets of newspaper; and a rock (to weigh down the bag). First, cut 3 to 4 inches off the top of the bag. (Save this piece to use as a fence or roof shingles.) Decorate the bag, then place crumpled newspaper and the rock inside. Attach a 5- by-5-inch piece of black construction paper to the top of the bag to form a roof; glue in place. Finally, place the houses in a row, or add tombstones for a spooky cemetery scene.   Shirley Bullard

Pumpkin Pals

Try a new twist when decorating your classroom and school by using real pumpkins and vegetables. Make a witch by putting a black witch's hat made of rolled black poster board on top of the pumpkin. Stick the end of a cucumber into a hole in the pumpkin to make a long nose. Attach a cherry tomato to the end of the cucumber with a toothpick for a wart.

Make a creature from outer space! First, roll a tube from a sturdy piece of cardboard and staple. Then place the pumpkin on top of the cardboard tube for the head. The cardboard tube serves as the creature's body. Cut feet from construction paper and glue or staple to body. Poke lollipops through body for arms. Cucumbers protruding from holes carved in pumpkin form nose and eyes. Place a red pepper in the mouth for a tongue. Bend lollipop sticks and insert into the top of the pumpkin for antennae.

Michael G. L. McDaniel and Mary F. MacDonald

NOVEMBER

Turkeys turn up in many disguises this month. Paper strips, bags, fabric samples, and cornhusks are just some of the raw materials that reappear as gobblers.

Other November projects include bookmarks, dioramas, and storybook houses to honor Children's Book Week.

Pine-Cone Palaces

Cover small boxes (from toothpaste, vitamins, or beauty soap) with brown paper cut from paper bags. Then glue boxes together to suggest a castle. Insert large pine-cone towers in small holes cut in boxes with craft knife. Edge holes with glue to steady cones. Glue smaller cones and petals in place. Use cones from a white pine tree to get individual petals or scales that can be easily broken from the cone and trimmed with scissors. For large tower roofs, make brown paper cones. Glue petals in circles for smaller roofs. Add doors and windows with marking pen.

Giant Mosaic

On a large piece of paper, sketch a design. Using different colored markers, indicate what color each section should be on the paper. Divide the paper into sections with a pencil. There should be one section for each student to work on. Number the sections on the back of the paper. Then cut them apart. Cut colored construction paper into half-inch squares. Each child glues the colored squares into the proper area of his or her section of the mosaic. Tape the sections together when students are finished for a project the class can be proud of.

Christie Costanzo

Folded-Paper Rabbit

Remember: Always use absolutely square paper. Novice folders should letter both sides of the paper to correspond to the lettering in the diagram. **1.** Fold square in half vertically (GH). Unfold. Fold in half horizontally (EF) and unfold. Fold point A to point D, creating diagonal CB. Unfold and fold point B to point C, making the diagonal AD. Unfold. These four folds are "helping" folds, made to crease the paper so that subsequent folds will be easier. **2.** Fold line AC to GH, and then fold BD to GH. **3.** Fold A and B down to lie on horizontal line EF. **4.** Place thumbs inside two corner pockets and pull points A and B outward and down to make triangular points. (Be sure to check with illustration No. 4.) **5.** From top point O of centerfold make diagonal folds to points A and B. **6.** Fold bottom corners back. **7.** Fold model in half (reversing centerfold). **8.** Fold tail inward (a "squash fold"). Push thumb into point to keep the fold even and pinch the sides together. *Rabbit is taken from* Papercrafts *by Ian Adair (David and Charles Holdings, Ltd., 1975).*

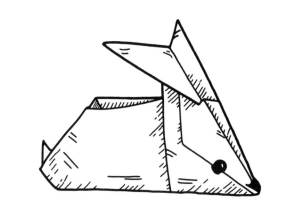

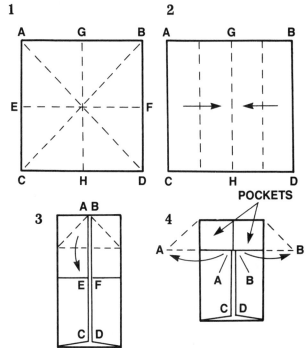

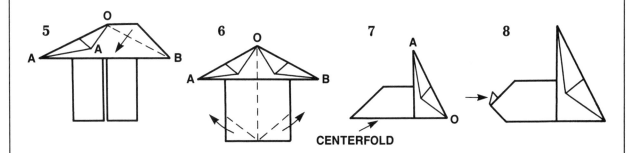

• *See page 70 for additional paper-folding materials.*

Pattern Art

Patterns don't have to prohibit creativity. It depends on the way they are used. We made the paper art here by adapting two circle patterns (one 5½ inches in diameter and one 3½ inches). Children traced around poster-board patterns and cut out the number of construction-paper circles they needed to make their selected figures. Circles were sometimes cut in half (ladybug wings), sometimes folded in half (robin body, wings, and tail). Triangle-like shapes were used for the fish tail and pig ears. Crayons, markers, and paper scraps added detail.   Jane Armstrong

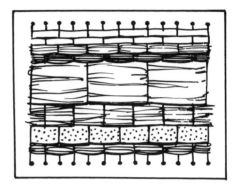

Cardboard Loom Weaving

Cut large rectangular openings in pieces of heavy cardboard. On the back of each cardboard, mark where two rows of evenly spaced holes will go at opposite ends of your frame. Poke the holes through the cardboard with a large needle. With a smaller needle, run colored strings between the rows. Students can create interesting designs by weaving yarn, fabric strips, ribbon, raffia, dried grasses, and grains.

Joan Lunich Schenk

Space Scenes

Add special interest to space drawings or cut-paper scenes with some 3-D touches. Foil-covered egg-carton sections make good space creatures visiting here from an outer space planet.   James Perrin

Mitten Hand Puppets

The thumb is the creature's lower jaw and the palm its open mouth. Add button, sequin, yarn features. A person wearing a pair of mittens made into two different creatures can produce a solo puppet show.

Peanut Puppets

Unshelled peanuts make intriguing finger puppets. Cut a hole in one end to get out the peanut and make a place for the finger to fit. Add features with felt pen, make clothing by tying a square of fabric around the peanut's "middle," and your puppet is ready to perform.

Brown-Bag Tote

Insert one grocery bag inside another for double strength. Fold about a 6-inch cuff to the inside. Use plastic handles cut from a thin plastic shopping bag and attach them to front and back of bag by sewing through the paper bag and over the handle repeatedly. Thread a strong needle with a double strand of yarn. Crayon and cut out pictures of things that might be carried in a bag. Paste to outside. If plastic handles are hard to find, reinforce top of bag with tape, punch holes, and use braided yarn.

Native American Writing

The Native Americans had many uses for bear skins: shelters, clothes, blankets. Often they wrote messages on these skins, using symbols inspired by familiar things. Students can make "bearskins" by tearing brown bags into the shape of a bear skin, crumpling it, and then smoothing it out. They then use Native American signs or their own symbols to write a message on their skins.

Marian Hostetler

• *See page 70 for reference materials on Native American crafts.*

Hanger Weaving

A good loom for weaving in upper grades is a wire coat hanger bent into a new form. The warp (lengthwise threads) is strung across the indentations of the hanger and tied securely. Weaving can be done easily by hand. Students can use all kinds of yarns and other materials to create unusual weaving patterns. Tassels, fringes, or bows make interesting accents. When finished, the hanger hook makes displaying the completed work easy.

Joan Mary Macey

Paper-Bag Puppet Heads

Stuff a small paper bag, insert stick or wooden spoon into bag, and tie tightly. Paint on features and decorate with yarn, construction paper, cloth. Large paper ears, nose, or a trunk will turn bags into realistic animal heads. Real hats or caps pinned in place will add a jaunty air.

Inviting Invitations

To help increase attendance at P.T.A. meetings or at school open houses during American Education Week, have children take home clever hand-crafted invitations. Here are five examples you might use as "starters."

After a short discussion of possible catch phrases, let each child develop an idea, choosing a favorite technique. Have various media available (tempera, crayon, pastels, cut paper, India ink, and so on), and let children search the class scrap box for materials.

Open-House Children

It looks as if class is in session when parents find each seat in the classroom occupied by a paper-plate child. Students paint backs of two fluted paper plates. Staple plates together after inserting a wire coat hanger between them. Add construction paper features, yarn for hair, etc. Bend hangers to a diamond shape. Have children bring a dress or shirt to slip over the "person" fastened to the seat with masking tape. Make arms from 12-by-18-inch construction paper by tracing children's arms and hands. Pin hands and arms into garment sleeves. Make a version of yourself, too. Violet Johnson

• *Get ready for American Education Week open houses with these projects.*

Oatmeal-Box Animals

Try making some offbeat animals with your class. First, obtain enough cardboard oatmeal canisters for half of your class. Then cut them in half vertically and give each student a half. Cut out wings, fins, horns, tails, and beaks. Hand out cardboard, glue, construction paper, and decoration materials and let the children start making animals. Some past successes have included dinosaurs, turtles, dogs, and dragons. These creatures make adorable figures and can be used to act out a favorite book or in dramatic play about animals.

Joel A. Nelson

- *These projects tie in well with National Children's Book Week.*

Personal Bookplates

Generate interest in books during National Children's Book Week by having a bookplate project. Explain that bookplates not only identify a book's owner but reflect that person's personality. Have children fold a large sheet of paper into small rectangles and then let them work on creating many different designs. They can paste or tape their favorite designs on the inside covers of some of the books they own.

Beverly Hill

Clothespin Bookmarks

In honor of National Children's Book Week, make clothespin bookmarks. Cut book shapes from colored paper. Write the name of a favorite story or draw a favorite character on the front. Glue the back of the shape to a wooden clip clothespin.

Storybook Houses

For each storybook display you'll need a brown-paper lunch bag, a 9-by-12-inch piece of heavy cardboard, felt-tip markers, multicolored sheets of oak tag, tissue paper, and a sheet of newspaper. First, affix the bottom of the paper bag to the center of the cardboard and stuff it with crumpled newspaper. Next, fold over the top of the bag, staple in place, and attach a construction-paper roof. Decorate the exterior of the house (door, windows, walkway, garden) with markers, small pieces of oak tag, and tissue paper. Add cutout characters for a finishing touch.

Connie Gatley

- *Try these projects during National Children's Book Week.*

Book Diorama

Once upon a time there was a colorful book diorama. . . . For each one you'll need a cigar box, a 9-by-12-inch sheet of white paper, construction paper, felt-tip markers, fabric scraps, and yarn. To transform the box into a book, cover the top, sides, and bottom with white paper. Draw horizontal lines along the edges to resemble a book's pages. Decorate the outside of the box with markers and construction paper; inside, attach cutout characters. Adorn the characters with fabric scraps, yarn, and buttons. Print a familiar quote from the book on the inside cover. Group the dioramas together and proudly display them in your classroom during National Children's Book Week.

Connie Gatley

Basic-Shape Pilgrims

Design Pilgrim people from simple, familiar shapes. Add cut-paper objects to represent the important daily occupations of pioneer life. Make the Pilgrim figures as large as possible from sheets of colored construction paper. Use tape to mount them on locker doors, along an empty wall, or under a chalkboard.

For an interesting mural, first crayon or paint a scene with forests, fields, cabins, and a church. Then paste figures on this background. Native Americans and animal figures could also be added for a bulletin-board display.

Handfuls of Thanks

Have children trace both their hands on light-colored construction paper. Print the word *Thanksgiving* across each hand. Ask the children to write on each finger one person or thing they are thankful for. Then they can decorate the rest of each hand. Cut out the hands and display pairs on the bulletin board. When Thanksgiving vacation arrives, take down the hands so students will have their own handfuls of thanks to take home and share with the family.   Cheryl Bogrow

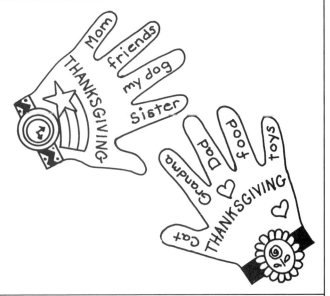

Corn Cluster

Cut two orange or yellow paper ears of corn and staple together with tissue between for stuffing. Use crayons to draw in kernels. Fasten clusters of about seven ears to husks cut from strips of brown paper bags. Hang several corn clusters as Thanksgiving decorations.   Ireene Robbins

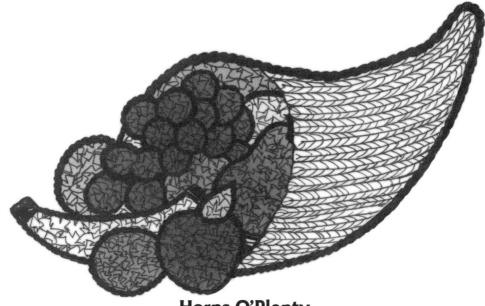

Horns O'Plenty

Draw a large cornucopia on paper and cover its exterior with bright yellow yarn. Add a harvest of fruit, and outline both the fruit and the horn with black yarn. Fill in the fruit with crumpled balls of colored tissue paper.   Jay Scott

Turkey Cups

Cut off three sides of the top of a small milk carton. Cover the outside of the carton including the remaining side of the top with foil. Glue pressed leaves in a fan shape (feathers) to the remaining side of the top. Add turkey features and fill with goodies.   Eleanor Hartmann

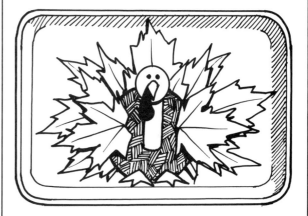

Turkey Trays

Set out leaves, plastic foam trays, and construction paper. Make turkeys by gluing arrangements of real leaves for feathers onto construction-paper bodies. Then glue bodies onto trays. Draw in features.   Jay Scott

Pilgrim Hats

Use white plastic foam drinking cups to make Pilgrim hats. Place cups on a flat cookie sheet. Put into a preheated oven at 350 degrees for 12–15 seconds. The cups will shrink to look like miniature hats. Let students decorate with paint, ribbon, and foil. These little hats make great party favors.

Jeanne Jewkes

Paper-Plate Turkeys

Ribbed paper plates can be turned into turkey tails. Notch the edge of plate, as shown. Or slit it into an uneven number of "spokes" and weave around them with odds and ends of yarn, string, or crepe-paper strips. Paste on colored-paper details and paint feathers.

Fan-Tailed Turkey

To make this quick-as-can-be Thanksgiving turkey, you'll need construction paper, heavy cardboard, and felt-tip markers. First, cut out the turkey's body from cardboard, then make a beak and legs from construction paper and attach them to the turkey. Next, fold five sheets of construction paper fan-style and glue each one, side by side, to the back of the turkey. Draw in feathers and add button eyes.

Athena Lynch

Loopy Thanksgiving Turkey

Cut paper strips about 3 inches wide. Use brown for the body and head; orange for beak; red for wattle; yellow, blue, green, orange, and red for the tail. Tail and head pieces are about 12 inches long; beak and wattle pieces about 6 inches; and body about 14 inches. Form the body loop, then make tail pieces into loops and staple close together on the body. Attach head loop opposite tail. Add the wattle so it hangs below the head; accordion-fold beak with four folds and add to head. Last of all add cut-paper eyes and yarn legs and feet. Hang from ceiling.

Carol McRoberts

Dressed Turkeys

Have your students make "turkeys with dressing" to decorate your classroom. Children cut out turkey bodies from brown construction paper and add clothing cut from fabric scraps and wallpaper books.

Barbara Gribben

Hanger Pilgrims

Holding the hook of a wire coat hanger with one hand, pull the bottom of the hanger out into a diamond shape. Cut one leg from a pair of panty hose, pull it over the hanger, and tie it at each end with a piece of string. Cut away the extra material. Glue on buttons and pipe cleaners for facial features. Cut Pilgrim hats, hair, and collars from construction paper and glue on.

Sylvia Albert

Thanksgiving Friends

Design Native American and Pilgrim faces from paper plates. Cut double hat shapes and fasten together at the edges (or fold circular brims in half) to allow them to fit over the top of the plate. (Trim plate slightly, if necessary.) Paste on yarn hair and construction-paper features.

Mosaic Corn

Glue multicolored paper bits to construction-paper corn shapes. Cut out paper husks and staple in place. Make a bow from shiny paper or ribbon and glue on. Send home or use to decorate the classroom or a hallway.

Sister Gwen Floryance

Fabric Turkey

A fabric sample cut from a discarded upholstery book provides this bird with a textured body. Give students an exercise in coordinating colors by having the fabric or paper used for their turkeys' feathers, heads, and feet complement the colors of the body.

Joan Lunich Schenk

Jumbo Turkey

The body of this gobbler is a supersized paper wad. Have each student crumble and pack newspaper into a football-sized ball. Smooth colored tissue paper over the wad, overlapping the ends on one side. Now cut a 12-inch-wide semicircle for the tail, and glue the overlapped side of the wad to it. Add a paper head (with button eyes and paper beak) and feet, then fringe the tail and paint on feathers.   Joan Lunich Schenk

Turkey Dressing

Create turkeys with personality! Cut out paper bodies, then add attire fashioned from paper scraps, yarn, buttons, sequins, burlap, and lace.   Carole Hutcheson

Diorama Figures

Juice-can figures may be used in a sandbox scene or diorama.

For a Pilgrim hat, insert a pleated-paper nut cup in the cutout center of a cardboard circle. Native American blankets can be cut from patterned wallpaper or gift wrapping. Bits of gift ribbon combine for a brightly hued headdress.

Turkey in the Bag

Crayon bands of color around top of a paper bag, extending them almost to middle of bag. Cut this top into inch-wide strips. Stuff the uncolored half of bag and tie. Spread paper strips and trim to form turkey's tail. Add paper wings and head. Placed in a nest of fall leaves, this gobbler makes a perfect centerpiece.

Newsworthy Pilgrims

Draw simple Pilgrim figures with black markers on a sheet of newspaper. Cut and glue newspaper Pilgrims to black construction paper. Add white hats, collars, apron, and cuffs.

Candy Cook

Paper-Quilling Turkey

Narrow strips of colored paper are used in this adaptation of the old art of paper quilling. Give each student a shallow box lid on which to design a turkey. Then show children how to glue on a large circle as the body, filling it in with paper strips wound into tight tubes and coils. Form wings and tail feathers with longer loops.

Jay Hanlon

Handy Turkeys

In six flat trays put six colors of fingerpaint. Help each child press the palm of a hand into one color, then press on paper. Then students press, one at a time, each finger and thumb into other colors to make head and tail. They add details and the verse at right.

Amy Marotta and Christopher Boettcher

This isn't just a turkey
As anyone can see,
I made it with
     my hand,
Which is a part of me.
It comes with
     lots of love
Especially to say,
I hope you have a
VERY
HAPPY
THANKSGIVING
DAY
Sue

Pilgrim Puppet

Lunch bags make great hand puppets, and younger students will love these Pilgrim puppets at Thanksgiving. Place bag open side facing down. Cut out construction-paper features and costume and glue to bag. Glue Pilgrim's arms to side of bag.

Amy Marotta

Husky Turkey

Cornhusks give this fellow a tail with dimension. Use the husks in their natural color or tint with food coloring before gluing to the back of a paper bird. (Look for husks in the Mexican-food section of markets or in craft stores.) Joanna Hunt

Pine-Cone Turkeys

Cut short strips from red, tan, green, and brown construction paper. Put a dab of glue on each and slip into cone for feathers. Add construction-paper head to flat end of cone.　Barbara Greenfield

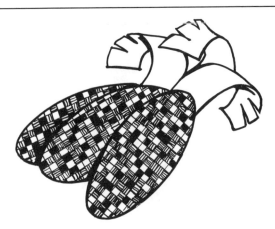

Turkey Totem

This turkey totem is drawn with markers on a long, narrow sheet of paper. Give students pictures of real totems for ideas, encouraging them to draw their turkeys turned in different directions, as the figures on real totems are. Cut out the finished totems and mount on paper.　James Perrin

Indian Corn

Students draw the shape of ears of corn on graph paper. They color each square in the shapes the colors of corn, pressing hard to get texture. Cut out and glue each ear to a brown wrapping-paper husk that is curled to look authentic. Use to decorate Thanksgiving bulletin boards.　Marcia Buechel

Masking-Tape Vases

For each vase you'll need a small glass bottle or jar, masking tape, premixed paint, and liquid detergent. First, tear masking tape into small, irregularly shaped pieces. Attach the pieces to the bottle, overlapping slightly. When entire bottle is covered with tape, coat with a mixture of paint and liquid detergent. Mist bottle with clear acrylic spray. Add a masking-tape bow—two strips of tape, sticky sides together—as a finishing touch. Send home as Thanksgiving centerpieces.

Julie Stempinski

Turkey in Disguise

Here's a tom turkey who's decided to wear the disguise of a Pilgrim, perhaps to avoid coming to Thanksgiving dinner *as* dinner! For a humorous approach to the annual feast day, have students draw turkeys in human attire. What celebrities might their birds "dress" as?

James Perrin

Thanksgiving Place Mats

Have students cut brown bags into 16-by-11-inch rectangles and fringe with scissors. Using crayons, paper cutouts, and other materials, they personalize each one for family members.

Carolyn Wilhelm

Resources

Clay Resource Kit

A clay resource kit is available on loan. Send a postcard requesting *Pottery #26* to:
Extension Program, National Gallery of Art, Washington, DC 20565

Native American Crafts

These books contain examples of authentic Native American art:
The Art of the Southwest Indians by Shirley Glubok (Macmillan, 1978)
Indian Crafts and Lore by Ben W. Hunt (Golden Press, 1976)
Indian Picture Writing by Robert Hofsinde (Morrow, 1959)

Art Activities to Help Children Communicate

Tell Me About Your Picture: Art Activities to Help Children Communicate by Janet Carson (Prentice-Hall, 1984)

Quilting

Suggested books that focus on quilting:

Fiction
The Josefina Story Quilt by Eleanor Coerr (Harper & Row, 1986)
The Patchwork Quilt by Valerie Flournoy (Dial Books for Young Readers, 1985)
The Quilt Story by Tony Johnston and Tomie dePaola (G.P. Putnam's Sons, 1985)

Nonfiction
Great American Quilts (Oxmoor House, 1988)
101 Patchwork Patterns by Ruby McKim (Dover, 1962)
The Standard Book of Quilt Making and Collecting by Marguerite Ickis (Dover, 1949)

Masks

Good resources for pictures include the following:
Dancing Masks of Africa by Christine Price (Scribners, 1975)
Masks of Black Africa by Ladislas Segy (Dover, 1975)
Masks and Mask Makers by Kari Hunt and Bernice Carlson (Abingdon, 1961)

Paper Folding

Books that include other paper-folding projects:
Elementary Art Games and Puzzles by Florence Temko (Parker/Prentice-Hall, 1982)
Paper Dreams by Lorraine Bodger (Universe Books, 1977)

Thanksgiving

For more information on historically true customs and costumes:
If You Sailed on the Mayflower by Ann McGovern (Scholastic Book Services, 1975)
Pilgrim Children on the Mayflower by Ida DeLage (Garrard, 1981)
Turkeys, Pilgrims, and Indian Corn by Edna Barth (Clarion Books, 1975)

Columbus Day

For background information on Columbus:
A Book About Christopher Columbus by Ruth Belov Gross (Scholastic Book Services, 1974)
Christopher Columbus by Ann McGovern (Scholastic Book Services, 1962)